I Can Be Anything!

I CAN BE A FIREFIGHTER

By Audrey Charles

Please visit our website, www.garethstevens.com. For a free color catalog of all our high-quality books, call toll free 1-800-542-2595 or fax 1-877-542-2596.

Cataloging-in-Publication Data

Names: Charles, Audrey.
Title: I can be a firefighter / Audrey Charles.
Description: New York : Gareth Stevens Publishing, 2018. | Series: I can be anything! | Includes index.
Identifiers: ISBN 9781482463217 (pbk.) | ISBN 9781482463231 (library bound) | ISBN 9781482463224 (6 pack)
Subjects: LCSH: Fire fighters–Juvenile literature. | Fire extinction–Juvenile literature.
Classification: LCC TH9148.C43 2018 | DDC 628.9′2–dc23

First Edition

Published in 2018 by
Gareth Stevens Publishing
111 East 14th Street, Suite 349
New York, NY 10003

Editor: Therese Shea
Designer: Sarah Liddell

Photo credits: Cover, p. 1 (kid) Rido/Shutterstock.com; cover, p. 1 (background) Mariusz S. Jurgielewicz/Shutterstock.com; p. 5 Johnny Habell/Shutterstock.com; p. 7 Ron Hilton/Shutterstock.com; p. 9 Keith Muratori/Shutterstock.com; pp. 11, 24 (hose) Ron Frank/Shutterstock.com; pp. 13, 24 (ladder) Elnur/Shutterstock.com; pp. 15, 24 (ax) Flashon Studio/Shutterstock.com; p. 17 Monkey Business Images/Shutterstock.com; pp. 19, 21 Hero Images/Getty Images; p. 23 Ariel Skelley/Getty Images.

Printed in the United States of America

CPSIA compliance information: Batch #CS17GS: For further information contact Gareth Stevens, New York, New York at 1-800-542-2595.

Contents

Fighting Fires and More . . . 4
Meet Jim 18
Let's Be Firefighters! 22
Words to Know 24
Index. 24

Firefighters put out fires.

They wear a hat,
coat, and boots.
These keep them safe
from heat.

Firefighters drive
a red truck.
It's called an engine.

ONLY
E. BALTIMORE
TRUCK 2
TRUCK 2
FIRE DEPARTMENT
TRUCK
2

They use a hose.
It carries water.

They climb tall ladders!

They use axes.
Axes can cut down doors!

Firefighters also help people who are hurt.

This is Jim.
He's a firefighter!

Jim teaches kids
about fire.
He tells them how
to be safe.

I can be
a firefighter, too.
So can you!

FIRE
CHIEF
FIRE
EXTINGUISHER

Words to Know

ax

hose

ladder

Index

axes 14
hat 6
hose 10
ladders 12
wear 6